- The Treaty establishing a Constitution for Europe was signed in Rome on 29 October 2004 by the Heads of State or Government of the twenty-five Member States.
- The European Constitution will come into force on 1 November 2006 if it is ratified by the 25 Member States of the European Union, either in parliament or by referendum.
- In January 2005, the European Parliament voted in favour of the Treaty establishing a Constitution for Europe by 500 votes to 137, with 40 abstentions.

Dear European citizens,

The European Parliament is delighted to welcome you here today as one of the thousands of visitors we receive every year.

I hope your visit to our institution will give you an insight into the day-to-day work of the MEPs you have elected.

Your visit comes at a time when the European Union is preparing to adopt a Constitution and when the European Parliament has given its overwhelming backing to the project by approving the Corbett – Méndez de Vigo report.

Marking a major step towards a political Europe, this Constitution is first and foremost about you. It enshrines your fundamental rights, both civil and political, and the democratic values on which the European Union is founded. Furthermore, it provides the basis for the European Union to speak with a single voice in the world.

If it is ratified by the national parliaments or by the people of the 25 Member States its adoption will consolidate our 50 years of European history and lead our Union into a stage of maturity.

This publication aims to provide you with all the information you need to participate actively in a debate which will determine the future of the Union and, therefore, your future.

Borrell

Josep BORRELL FONTELLES
President of the European Parliament

CONTENTS

7. Acts and procedures: a more coherent, precise and comprehensible system
8. The Union's finances
9. Progress on sectoral policies
    - *The Area of Freedom, Security and Justice*
    - *Other internal policies*
    - *Common foreign and security policy*
    - *Other areas of external relations*
10. A significant degree of flexibility
11. Entry into force of the Constitution

- *Overall assessment/recommendation to approve the Constitution*

European Parliament resolution on the Treaty establishing a Constitution for Europe (2004/2129(INI))

The European Parliament,

- having regard to the Treaty establishing a Constitution for Europe (hereinafter 'the Constitution'),
- having regard to the Treaty on European Union and the Treaty establishing the European Community as amended by the Single European Act and the Treaties of Maastricht, Amsterdam and Nice,
- having regard to the Charter of Fundamental Rights of the European Union[1],
- having regard to the European Council's Laeken Declaration[2],
- having regard to its resolutions[3] paving the way towards a Constitution for Europe,
- having regard to its resolutions[4] preparing past intergovernmental conferences and its resolutions[5] assessing their outcome,
- having regard to the draft Treaty establishing a Constitution for Europe adopted by consensus by the European Convention on 13 June and 10 July 2003, as well as its resolutions[6] preparing and subsequently assessing the work of the Convention,
- having regard to the opinions on the Constitution delivered by the Committee of the Regions on 17 November 2004[7] and the European Economic and Social Committeeon 28 October 2004[8] at the request of the European Parliament[9],
- having regard to the views expressed by the representatives of regional associations, social partners and platforms of civil society at a public hearing convened on 25 November 2004,
- having regard to Rule 45 of its Rules of Procedure,
- having regard to the report of the Committee on Constitutional Affairs and the opinions of the Committee on Foreign Affairs, the Committee on Development, the Committee on International Trade, the Committee on Budgets, the Committee on Budgetary Control, the Committee on Employment and Social Affairs, the Committee on the Environment, Public Health and Food Safety, the Committee

on Industry, Research and Energy, the Committee on Regional Development, the Committee on Agriculture, the Committee on Fisheries, the Committee on Legal Affairs, the Committee on Civil Liberties, Justice and Home Affairs and the Committee on Petitions (A6-0070/2004),

Whereas:

A. the European Union has, in the course of its history, played a substantial role in creating a continuously expanding area of peace and prosperity, democracy and freedom, justice and security,

B. the Constitution consolidates these achievements and brings about innovations which are essential to maintaining and enhancing the capacity of the Union of twenty-five and potentially more Member States to act effectively internally and externally,

C. the efforts to achieve a Constitution deployed by the European Parliament since its first direct election, have been crowned by the success of the Convention, which prepared the draft using a democratic, representative and transparent method that has fully proved its effectiveness, and which took account of the contributions of the citizens of Europe, resulting in a consensus which was left essentially unchanged by the Intergovernmental Conference,

D. the Constitution, as a compromise that had to be acceptable to all Member States, inevitably left out some proposals, notably of the European Parliament and of the Convention, that would have, in the view of their authors, brought further improvements to the Union, many of which remain possible in the future,

E. the agreement to the Constitution of every single national government in the European Union demonstrates that the elected governments of Member States all consider that this compromise is the basis on which they wish to work together in the future, and will require each of them to demonstrate maximum political commitment to ensuring ratification by 1 November 2006,

F. the Constitution has been the object of some criticism voiced in public debate that does not reflect the real content and legal consequences of its provisions, insofar as the Constitution will not lead to the creation of a centralised superstate, will strengthen rather than weaken the Union's social dimension and does not ignore the historical and spiritual roots of Europe since it refers to its cultural, religious and humanist inheritance,

1. Concludes that, taken as a whole, the Constitution is a good compromise and a vast improvement on the existing treaties, which will, once implemented, bring about visible benefits for citizens (and the European Parliament and the national parliaments as their democratic representation), the Member States (including their regions and local authorities) and the effective functioning of the European Union institutions, and thus for the Union as a whole;

Greater clarity as to the Union's nature and objectives

2. Welcomes the fact that the Constitution provides citizens with more clarity as to the Union's nature and objectives and as to the relations between the Union and the Member States, notably because:

   (a) the complex set of European treaties is replaced by a single more readable document spelling out the objectives of the Union, its powers and their limits, its policy instruments and its institutions;

   (b) the Union's dual legitimacy is reaffirmed, and it is clarified that it is a Union of States and citizens;

   (c) the canon of values common to all the Member States, on which the Union is founded and which creates a strong bond between the Union's citizens, is made explicit and widened;

   (d) the objectives of the Union as well as the principles governing its action and its relations with Member States are clarified and better defined;

   (e) economic, social and territorial cohesion is reaffirmed as an objective of the Union;

   (f) there are new provisions of general application concerning a high level of employment, the promotion of equality between women and men, the elimination of all kinds of discriminations, the fight against social exclusion and the promotion of social justice, social protection, a high level of education, training and health, the protection of the consumer, the promotion of sustainable development and the respect of services of general interest;

(g) the confusion between the «European Community» and «European Union» will end as the European Union becomes one single legal entity and structure;

(h) European legal acts are simplified and their terminology is clarified, using more understandable vocabulary: "European laws" and "European framework laws" replace the existing multiple types of act (regulations, directives, decisions, framework decisions, etc);

(i) it provides guarantees that the Union will never be a centralised all-powerful "superstate":

- the strong emphasis on decentralisation inherent in "united in diversity",
- the obligation to "respect the national identities of Member States, inherent in their fundamental structures, political and constitutional, inclusive of regional and local self-government",
- the principles of conferred powers (whereby the Union's only competences are those conferred on it by the Member States), subsidiarity and proportionality,
- the participation of the Member States themselves in the Union's decision-making system and in agreeing any changes to it;

(j) the inclusion of the symbols of the Union in the Constitution will improve awareness of the Union's institutions and their action;

(k) a solidarity clause between Member States provides citizens with an expectation of receiving support from all parts of the Union in case of a terrorist attack or a natural or man-made disaster;

Greater effectiveness and a strengthened role in the world

3. Welcomes the fact that, with the entry into force of the Constitution, the Union's institutions will be able to carry out their tasks more effectively, notably because:

(a) there is a significant increase in the areas in which the governments meeting in Council will decide by qualified majority voting rather than by unanimity, a vital factor if the Union of twenty-five Member States is to be able to function without being blocked by vetoes;

(b) the European Council will have a two-and-a-half-year chair instead of a six-month rotating one;

(c) there will, as of 2014, be a reduction in the number of members of the Commission based on an equal rotation between Member States;

(d) there will be a significant enhancement of the Union's visibility and capacity as a global actor:

- the European Union's Foreign policy High Representative and the Commissioner for External Relations - two posts causing duplication and confusion - will be merged into a single European Union Minister for Foreign Affairs, who will be a Vice President of the Commission and will chair the Foreign Affairs Council and be able to speak for the Union on those subjects where the latter has a common position,
- there will be a single external action service which must be connected as closely as possible with the Commission and result in the strengthening of Europe as a community,
- the conferral of legal personality, previously enjoyed by the European Community, on the Union will enhance its capacity to act in international relations and to be a party to international agreements,
- the Union's capacity to develop common structures in the field of security and defence policy will be reinforced, while ensuring the necessary flexibility to cater for differing approaches of Member States to such matters;

(e) the number of the Union's legislative instruments and the procedures for their adoption will be reduced; the distinction between legislative and executive instruments will be clarified;

(f) action in the area of justice and home affairs will be subject to more effective procedures, promising tangible progress with regard to justice, security and immigration issues;

(g) for a number of other matters, it will become easier to apply the successful Community method as soon as there is the political will to do so;

(h) there is more room for flexible arrangements when not all Member States are willing or able to go ahead with certain policies at the same time;

More democratic accountability

4. Welcomes the fact that citizens will have greater control over the European Union's action by increased democratic accountability, notably due to the following improvements:

(a) the adoption of all European Union legislation will be subject to the prior scrutiny of national parliaments and, with a few exceptions, the dual approval of both national governments (in the Council) and the directly elected European Parliament - a level of parliamentary scrutiny that exists in no other supranational or international structure;

(b) national parliaments will receive all European Union proposals in good time to discuss them with their ministers before the Council adopts a position and will also gain the right to object to draft legislation if they feel it goes beyond the European Union's remit;

(c) the European Parliament will as a rule decide on an equal footing with the Council on the Union's legislation;

(d) the President of the Commission will be elected by the European Parliament, thereby establishing a link to the results of European elections;

(e) the Union Minister for Foreign Affairs, appointed by the European Council in agreement with the Commission's

President, will be accountable both to the European Parliament and to the European Council;

(f) a new budgetary procedure will require the approval of both the Council and the European Parliament for all European Union expenditure, without exception, thus bringing all expenditure under full democratic control;

(g) the exercise of delegated legislative powers by the Commission will be brought under a new system of supervision by the European Parliament and the Council, enabling each of them to call back Commission decisions to which they object;

(h) agencies, notably Europol, will be subject to greater parliamentary scrutiny;

(i) the Council will meet in public when debating and adopting Union legislation;

(j) the role of the Committee of the Regions is reinforced;

(k) with regard to future revisions of the Constitution, the European Parliament, too, will have the power to submit proposals, and the scrutiny of any proposed revision must be carried out by a Convention unless Parliament agrees that this is not necessary;

More rights for citizens

5. Welcomes the fact that the rights of citizens will be strengthened as a result of the following improvements:

(a) the incorporation of the EU Charter of Fundamental Rights in Part II of the Constitution, which means that all provisions of European Union law and all action taken by the EU institutions or based on EU law will have to comply with those standards;

(b) the Union is to accede to the European Convention on Human Rights, thereby making the Union subject to the same external review as its Member States;

(c) new provisions will facilitate participation by citizens, the social partners, representative associations and civil society in the deliberations of the Union;

(d) the introduction of a European citizens' initiative, which will enable citizens to submit proposals on matters where they consider that a legal act of the Union is required in order to implement the Constitution;

(e) individuals will have greater access to justice in connection with European Union law;

Conclusions

6. Endorses the Constitutional Treaty and wholeheartedly supports its ratification;

7. Believes that this Constitution will provide a stable and lasting framework for the future development of the European Union that will allow for further enlargement while providing mechanisms for its revision when needed;

8. Announces its intention of using the new right of initiative conferred upon it by the Constitution to propose improvements to the Constitution;

9. Hopes that all Member States of the European Union will be in a position to achieve ratification by mid-2006;

10. Reiterates its request that all possible efforts be deployed in order to inform European citizens clearly and objectively about the content of the Constitution; therefore invites the European institutions and the Member States, when distributing the text of the constitutional Treaty to citizens (in unabridged or summary versions), to make a clear distinction between the elements already in force in the existing treaties and new provisions introduced by the Constitution, with a view to educating the public and informing the debate; invites them also to recognise the role of civil society organisations within the ratification debates and to make available sufficient support to enable such organisations to engage their constituencies in these debates across the EU in order to promote the active involvement of citizens in the discussions on ratification;

o

o o

11. **Instructs its President to forward this resolution and the report of the Committee on Constitutional Affairs to the national parliaments of the Member States, the Council, the Commission and the former Members of the European Convention, and to ensure that Parliament's services, including its Information Offices, provide ample information about the Constitution and Parliament's position on it.**

[1] OJ C 364, 18.12.2000, p.1.

[2] Laeken European Council, Laeken declaration on the future of the Union, SN 273/01, 15.12.2001.

[3] Resolution of 14.2.1984 on the draft Treaty establishing the European Union (OJ C 77, 19.3.1984, p. 5, rapporteur: Altiero Spinelli, 1-1200/1983).

Resolution of 11.7.1990 on the European Parliament's guidelines for a draft constitution for the European Union (OJ C 231, 17.9.1990, p. 91, rapporteur: Emilio Colombo, A3-0165/1990).

Resolution of 12.12.1990 on the constitutional basis of European Union (OJ C 19, 28.1.1991, p. 65, rapporteur: Emilio Colombo, A3-0301/1990).

Resolution of 10.2.1994 on the Constitution of the European Union (OJ C 61, 28.2.1994, p. 155, rapporteur: Fernand Herman, A3-0064/1994).

Resolution of 25.10.2000 on the constitutionalisation of the Treaties (OJ C 197, 12.7.2001, p. 186, rapporteur: Olivier Duhamel, A5-0289/2000).

[4] Resolution of 14.3.1990 on the Intergovernmental Conference in the context of Parliament's strategy for European Union (OJ C 96, 17.4.1990, p. 114, rapporteur: David Martin, A3-0047/1990).

Resolution of 11.7.1990 on the Intergovernmental Conference in the context of Parliament's strategy for European Union (OJ C 231, 17.9.1990, p. 97, rapporteur: David Martin, A3-0166/1990).

Resolution of 22.11.1990 on the Intergovernmental Conferences in the context of Parliament's strategy for European Union (OJ C 324, 24.12.1990, p. 219, rapporteur: David Martin, A3-0270/1990).

Resolution of 22.11.1990 embodying Parliament's opinion on the convening of the Intergovernmental Conferences on Economic and Monetary Union and on Political Union (OJ C 324, 24.12.1990, p. 238, rapporteur: David Martin, A3-0281/1990).

Resolution of 17.5.1995 on the functioning of the Treaty on European Union with a view to the 1996 Intergovernmental Conference - Implementation and development of the Union (OJ C 151, 19.6.1995, p. 56. rapporteurs: Jean-Louis Bourlanges and David Martin, A4-0102/1995).

Resolution of 13.3.1996 embodying (i) Parliament's opinion on the convening of the Intergovernmental Conference, and (ii) an evaluation of the work of the Reflection Group and a definition of the political priorities of the European Parliament with a view to the Intergovernmental Conference (OJ C 96, 1.4.1996, p. 77, rapporteurs : Raymonde Dury and Hanja Maij-Weggen, A4-0068/1996).

Resolution of 18.11.1999 on the preparation of the reform of the Treaties and the next Intergovernmental Conference (OJ C 189, 7.7.2000, p. 222, rapporteurs: Giorgos Dimitrakopoulos and Jo Leinen, A5-0058/1999).

Resolution of 3.2.2000 on the convening of the Intergovernmental Conference (OJ C 309, 27.10.2000, p. 85, rapporteurs: Giorgos Dimitrakopoulos and Jo Leinen, A5-0018/2000).

Resolution of 16.3.2000 on the drafting of a European Union Charter of Fundamental Rights (OJ C 377, 29.12.2000, p. 329, rapporteurs: Andrew Duff and Johannes Voggenhuber, A5-0064/2000).

Resolution of 13.4.2000 containing the European Parliament's proposals for the Intergovernmental Conference (OJ C 40, 7.2.2001, p. 409, rapporteurs: Giorgos Dimitrakopoulos and Jo Leinen, A5-0086/2000).

5 Resolution of 16.1.1986 on the position of the European Parliament on the Single Act approved by the Intergovernmental Conference on 16 and 17 December 1985 (OJ C 36, 17.2.1986, p. 144, rapporteur: Altiero Spinelli, A2-0199/1985).

Resolution of 11.12.1986 on the Single European Act (OJ C 7, 12.1.1987, p. 105, rapporteur: Luis Planas Puchades, A2-0169/1986).

Resolution of 7.4.1992 on the results of the Intergovernmental Conferences (OJ C 125, 18.5.1992, p. 81, rapporteurs: David Martin and Fernand Herman, A3-0123/1992).

Resolution of 19.11.1997 on the Amsterdam Treaty (OJ C 371, 8.12.1997, p. 99, rapporteurs: Iñigo Méndez de Vigo and Dimitris Tsatsos, A4-0347/1997).

Resolution of 31.5.2001 on the Treaty of Nice and the future of the European Union (OJ C 47 E, 21.2.2002, p. 108, rapporteurs: Iñigo Méndez de Vigo and António José Seguro, A5-0168/2001).

6 Resolution of 29.11.2001 on the constitutional process and the future of the Union (OJ C 153 E, 27.6.2002, p. 310, rapporteurs: Jo Leinen and Iñigo Méndez de Vigo, A5-0368/2001).

Resolution of 24.9.2003 on the draft Treaty establishing a Constitution for Europe and the European Parliament's opinion on the convening of the Intergovernmental Conference (OJ C 77 E, 26.3.2004, p. 255, rapporteurs: José María Gil-Robles Gil-Delgado and Dimitris Tsatsos, A5-0299/2003).

7 CdR 354/2003 fin, not yet published in the Official Journal.

8 CESE 1416/2004, not yet published in the Official Journal.

9 Items 8.2 and 8.3, P6_PV(2004)09-14.

EXPLANATORY STATEMENT

'I am not an advocate of frequent changes in laws and constitutions, but laws and institutions must go hand in hand with the progress of the human mind. As that becomes more developed, more enlightened, as new discoveries are made, new truths discovered, and manners and opinions change, with change of circumstances, institutions must advance also to keep pace with the times. We might as well require a man to wear still the coat which fitted him when a boy, as civilised society to remain ever under the regime of their ancestors.'

Thomas Jefferson

I. Introduction

1. More than half a century ago, the Schuman Declaration set in train an ambitious undertaking: that of uniting Europeans, who had been divided for centuries by fratricidal conflicts, around a common project.

Success was dependent on a resolution of the three crucial issues facing Europe at the end of the Second World War: how to overcome the internal demons which were the root cause of the most serious disasters to have affected our continent, how to regain a place at the forefront of world affairs, and how to develop economic conditions which would guarantee the survival of a stable democratic order.

The history of the last five decades is the chronicle of a success. Europe has managed to consolidate a political system based on the principles of freedom, pluralism and tolerance; has reconciled countries which had been enemies only just before, ushering in the longest period of peace in modern times; has secured for Europeans high levels of material well-being and social progress; has helped to bring about the dismantling of the Iron Curtain which divided the Europe of the free from the Europe of the oppressed. All these achievements of the European integration process should not lead us to forget its true objectives: making nationalist excesses, the real cancer affecting modern Europe, a thing of the past; defending democracy as a system which can channel divergent opinions in a pluralist society; and giving Europe a strong, influential voice to defend its ideas, its values and its interests.

However, Europe must not rest on its laurels: it must deal with the new challenges facing it at the start of the 21st century, i.e. the Union's role in international politics, globalisation, enlargement, the euro, the internal and external security of our continent, terrorism, migratory flows, education, technological progress, racism, xenophobia or social exclusion.

Since the first European Community (Coal and Steel: Paris Treaty of 18 April 1951[1]), which brought together six Western European countries[2], was established, the

European integration process has been extended to embrace 25 European States[3] and has seen its scope expand to cover new areas through the establishment of the Economic Community and the Atomic Energy (Euratom) Community (Treaties of Rome of 25 March 1957[4]) and, subsequently, the European Union (Maastricht Treaty of 7 February 1992).

2. Ever since the first European elections by universal suffrage in 1979, Parliament has consistently sought to democratise and make more effective and transparent the workings of what was to become the European Union. By adopting, on 14 February 1984, the first draft Treaty establishing the European Union (known as the 'Spinelli' draft, after its rapporteur), Parliament initiated a reform process which was to continue for the following 20 years and lead to the drafting of the Single European Act[5], the Maastricht Treaty[6], the Treaty of Amsterdam[7], the Treaty of Nice[8] and, now, the Treaty establishing a Constitution for Europe[9].

At each stage, with the Committee on Institutional Affairs, which in 1999 became the Committee on Constitutional Affairs, providing the driving force, Parliament played an active part in the preparatory talks and assessed the outcome of the various Intergovernmental Conferences (IGCs)[10].

Right from the start of this process, it advocated clarifying and enhancing the constitutional basis for the European Union, a need which became more and more acute under the pressure of successive enlargements, given their capacity to jeopardise the political dimension of the integration process.

Three distinct but related objectives have been pursued by Parliament to this end:

First, it has sought to clarify and where necessary strengthen the competences and responsibilities of the European Union itself. Parliament has consistently argued that powers should be attributed to, and exercised by, the Union on the basis of the 'principle of subsidiarity', i.e. it should exercise those responsibilities - but only those responsibilities - that can be carried out more effectively by common policies than by the Member States acting separately.

Second, it has argued that responsibilities exercised at European level should be carried out more effectively. Parliament was particularly critical of the practice of unanimity in the Council, arguing that, where it has been agreed to run a policy jointly, it makes no sense to give a blocking power to each of the component States of the Union. It has also pleaded for a stronger role to be given to the Commission in carrying out policies once they have been agreed, subject to proper scrutiny and control.

Third, it has made the case for better democratic control and accountability at European level. Those responsibilities which national parliaments, in ratifying the Treaties, have transferred to the Union should not be exercised by the Council (i.e.

national ministers) alone. The loss of parliamentary powers at the national level should be offset by an increase in parliamentary power at European level.

In the light of the mixed and clearly inadequate results achieved by the Treaties of Amsterdam and Nice, when set against the challenge posed by the doubling in the number of Member States, but also that of the further deepening of the Union, it became more and more apparent that the established method of revising the Treaties was no longer able to provide genuine responses to the issues raised by the development of Europe.

Parliament had already reached that conclusion, and outlined it clearly, in its resolution of 19 November 1997 (based on the report by Íñigo Méndez de Vigo and Dimitris Tsatsos, *see footnote 10 above*) which marked the real starting point of the political review process which was to culminate, in 1999, in the establishment, at the instigation of the German Council Presidency, of the Convention model, one first employed in connection with the drafting of the Charter of Fundamental Rights of the European Union.

The signatories to the Treaty of Nice, being aware of its imperfections, in fact annexed to it a Declaration No 23 'on the future of the Union'[11] which paved the way for further reform of the treaties, originally scheduled for 2004. This reform was to be prepared for by 'wide-ranging discussions with all interested parties: representatives of national parliaments and all those reflecting public opinion (...) representatives of civil society, etc.', which was to take place in 2001 with a view to the adoption of a declaration 'containing appropriate initiatives for the continuation of this process' at the European Council in Laeken.

3. Parliament, for its part, after having sought to work in partnership with the national parliaments, during the preparations for successive IGCs[12], was the first to propose[13], on the basis of the precedent set when the Charter of Fundamental Rights of the European Union was drawn up[14], the convening of a Convention comprising representatives of the Heads of State and Government of the Member States, the national parliaments and the European Parliament and the Commission and with the involvement, as full members, of representatives of the governments and parliaments of the applicant States.

The Convention on the Charter of Fundamental Rights demonstrated that a body of this kind was able to prepare a draft text likely to secure the approval of the Heads of State or Government. The open and transparent nature of the Convention and the quality of its debates had also facilitated efforts to achieve a consensus by giving every representative the opportunity, first of all, to express his or her own views, and, subsequently, to understand those of the other representatives.

The Laeken European Council of 14 and 15 December 2001, by adopting the 'Laeken declaration on the future of European Union'[15] followed up this initiative by setting out the organisational arrangements for the work of the Convention and, above all, defining its terms of reference and the issues that it would be called upon to discuss. Thus, the Convention on the Future of Europe (chairman: Valéry Giscard d'Estaing; vice-chairmen: Giuliano Amato and Jean-Luc Dehaene) was given the task of drawing up a preliminary draft Constitution to serve as the basis for the work of the IGC which was to follow.

The outcome of the Convention confirmed that the choice of this method had been a wise one, since the latter succeeded in presenting, after 16 months' work, a consensus-based text informed by intense debates which also drew on close dialogue with civil society.

For its part, Parliament, through the work of its Committee on Constitutional Affairs, exerted a major influence on the draft constitutional Treaty[16], only a very few provisions of which would be modified by the IGC. At that IGC, for the first time Parliament was fully involved in the proceedings, in the persons of its President, Pat Cox, and its two representatives, Íñigo Méndez de Vigo, subsequently replaced by Elmar Brok, and Klaus Hänsch.

II. How does the Constitution represent a step forward by comparison with the Treaties in force and, hence, the existing *acquis*?

The new Constitution proposed for the European Union includes a high number of significant reforms and improvements to the current Constitution (i.e. the set of overlapping treaties that currently serve as the de facto constitution). It is, of course, a compromise that is cautious in a number of respects. But it is a compromise that takes Europe forward, that has been elaborated after lengthy, public and pluralistic debates in the European Convention and has been finalised and approved by the elected governments of all 25 Member States - each of which wants this to be the basis on which they will work together in Europe in the future.

1. *A constitutional Treaty for the Union*

1.1. The question is sometimes raised as to whether the new document is a Constitution or a Treaty. A sterile debate on an issue which is nothing more than a red herring must be avoided: there is no doubt that, in formal terms, the document is a treaty which will be adopted and ratified in accordance with the rules in force governing the revision of treaties. There is no other possible procedure. However, by virtue of its nature and substance, this Treaty establishes a genuine Constitution.

1.2. The Constitutional Treaty defines the nature of the actions which the European Union (EU) may take and the values and principles which guide those actions; it describes the Union's competences; it lays down what institutions the EU will have, outlines its decision-making procedures, stipulates what form its acts will take; it defines citizens' rights vis-à-vis the EU; it lays down the rules governing its own revision, etc. This is the role of a constitution: laying down the conditions governing, and the limits to, the exercise of power in the context of a political entity and safeguarding citizens' rights.

1.3. To a substantial extent, the same is true of the existing Treaties: the Union already has its Constitution, deriving from the Treaties which brought it into being, just like any other political entity. By simplifying those Treaties, by giving them a more readily comprehensible structure, and by conferring on them a particularly formal status, a vital step has been taken towards clarifying the system with a view to making it more transparent and comprehensible for citizens.

1.4. On that basis, and despite the fears voiced in some quarters, endowing the Union with a Constitution in no way signifies that a first step has been taken towards the creation of a centralised 'superstate' which would inevitably sound the death knell for national States and irrevocably change the nature of the European Union (there are many examples of international organisations whose constituent act is rightly termed a constitution, including the International Labour Organisation (ILO), the World Health Organisation (WHO), or, one which is less frequently cited, the Universal Postal Union (UPU). Indeed, the reverse is true: as it stands, the Constitution can even be said to offer the Member States and Union citizens formal safeguards against Community action going too far.

1.5. It can legitimately be argued that Part III of the Constitutional Treaty should have been substantially revised and that many of its provisions are not truly constitutional in nature, are too detailed and complex and should have no place in a genuine Constitution. However, the remit conferred on the Convention did not cover such a task. Nevertheless, the degree of simplification is immediately evident: all the provisions have been brought together in a single coherent and structured document and a mere reading of Parts I and II, those which focus on the more specifically 'constitutional' aspects, is enough to provide members of the public with a clear and straightforward overview of the political reality of the Union and of their rights.

1.6. The length of Part III has given rise to the criticism that the Constitution is far too detailed and complex when compared to, for example, the US

Constitution. This is because Part III, like preceding treaties, spells out in detail, for each policy area, the objectives of EU action, thereby limiting it. There is no 'blank cheque' given to the EU institutions to act without restriction in any policy area.

2. *One single entity: the European Union*

2.1. A crucial step forward, in terms of transparency and understanding by citizens of the nature of the European project, has been taken by merging the various Treaties in a single document and by making a transition from a very complicated state of affairs, involving several overlapping entities (European Union, European Community), to a single entity, the European Union, endowed with a (single) legal personality at international level, which will increase the effectiveness and visibility of Union action at that level. At the same time, the three-pillar structure [common foreign and security policy (CFSP), justice and home affairs (JHA) and Community] has been done away with; all three have been merged into the single corpus of the Union, with a single institutional framework and the across-the-board application of the Community method, the sole exception being the common foreign and security policy (including defence), where specific decision-making procedures remain in force, as warranted by the specific nature of that policy area.

In short, therefore, the Constitution offers us a single Treaty, and a single entity: the European Union[17].

2.2. The Constitution lays down, in a prominent position (Article I-8), the *symbols of the Union*, i.e. its flag (a circle of 12 gold stars on a blue background), its anthem (the Ode to Joy from Beethoven's Ninth Symphony), its motto (United in Diversity), its currency (the euro) and Europe Day (9 May). These symbols are designed to enable citizens to identify more closely with and strengthen their feeling of belonging to a Community with a shared destiny.

3. *A clear definition of the Union's values, principles and objectives*

It is significant that the Constitution should open with articles defining the nature of the Union and the values and principles on which it is founded and the objectives which it is supposed to pursue by means of its action.

3.1. The very first article of the Constitution (Article I-1) enshrines the dual legitimacy of the Union, reflecting the will of the citizens and States of Europe. The Constitution places the emphasis on the individual, that is to say men and women with rights and duties who are citizens of the Union, through being citizens of a Member State, and who, by virtue of that fact, enjoy the additional set of rights afforded them by European citizenship.

This article sets out the founding principles of the European integration process: the Member States confer on the Union competences to attain objectives they have in common. At European level, the Union coordinates the policies by which the Member States aim to achieve these objectives, and it is the Union's institutions which exercise the competences conferred on it. At the same time, the Union undertakes to respect the national identity of the Member States, that is to say essential elements of their internal political structure. In this way the Union demonstrates its respect for the decisions which each Member State may take in relation to the geographical distribution of power - from the fixing of its frontiers to regional or local autonomy - the maintenance of public order and the safeguarding of national security. Lastly, the Constitution lays down the principle of loyal cooperation between the Union and its Member States with a view to achieving their shared objectives.

3.2. The constitutional foundations of the European Union must be firmly anchored to the values which underpin and must guide every action taken by its institutions.

In accordance with Article 2 of the Constitution, the values on which the entire European integration process is founded are respect for human dignity, freedom, democracy, equality, the rule of law and respect for human rights, including the rights of persons belonging to minorities. Moreover, these values represent the reference criteria governing future accessions and may serve as the basis for imposing sanctions on any Member States which violate them on a serious, persistent basis.

This article also defines the principles which guide the Union's action: pluralism, non-discrimination, tolerance, justice, solidarity and equality between women and men.

Finally, the Union pursues political objectives, objectives which justify its existence and which can be summarised as follows: the promotion of peace, the Union's values and the well-being of its peoples. They are given practical form in Article 3 of the Constitution in terms of political, economic and social objectives, as pursued within the Union and in the sphere of external relations.

Accordingly, at an internal level the Union offers it citizens an area of freedom, security and justice and an internal market based on free and fair competition. It works for the sustainable development of Europe, on the basis of balanced economic growth and price stability; to develop a highly competitive social market economy aiming at full employment and social progress; and to secure a high level of protection and improvement of the quality of the environment. It promotes scientific and technological advance. Finally, it combats social exclusion and all forms of discrimination and promotes social justice and protection, equality between men and women, solidarity between generations and the protection of the rights of the child. It promotes economic, social and territorial cohesion and solidarity among the Member States. It respects its rich cultural and linguistic diversity and ensures that Europe's cultural heritage is safeguarded and enhanced.

At an international level, the Union contributes to peace and security, the sustainable development of the Earth, solidarity and mutual respect among peoples, free and fair trade, the eradication of poverty and the protection of human rights, in particular the rights of the child, and to strict observance and the development of international law, in particular the United Nations Charter.

These objectives thus make up a basic political programme which was the well-spring for the establishment of the Union. It is incumbent on the Union to pursue these objectives by appropriate means, using the competences conferred on it in the Constitution.

The values and principles thus represent the ethical foundation of the Union, a foundation which is given practical form in the Charter of Fundamental Rights incorporated into Part II of the Constitution. The objectives assigned to it justify the existence of the Union and are the reason behind the Member States' decision to establish the Union. They govern its action in all areas. Although the values, principles and objectives defined in these articles are not entirely new, some of them had never previously been clearly stated and had never previously been codified and systematised. Codification of this kind is the hallmark of a Constitution and represents an important step towards providing citizens with a clear, highly symbolic insight into precisely what the Union signifies.

3.3. In that connection, it should be emphasised that the Intergovernmental Conference (IGC) essentially followed the text agreed on by the Convention, making only minor changes which Parliament can readily endorse: the addition to the list of values of the rights of persons belonging to minorities, the enshrinement of equality between women and men as a principle, the inclusion of 'price stability' among the Union's objectives, alongside that of the 'a highly competitive social market economy, aiming at full employment and social progress'.

4. *Citizens at the heart of the European integration process: the incorporation of the Charter of Fundamental Rights into the Constitution*

4.1. The incorporation of the Charter of Fundamental Rights into Part II of the Constitution signifies full acknowledgement of the fact that citizens are at the heart of the European integration process. As a result of this incorporation, the Charter has acquired binding legal force: it is thus binding both on the European institutions, acting in the framework of their respective competences, and on the Member States, but only when they act as implementers of Community law. It thus offers citizens an additional safeguard vis-à-vis the Union.

This in no way signifies that the protection of the fundamental rights guaranteed to citizens, vis-à-vis their States, by each national constitution is being called into question, or that competences are being surreptitiously conferred on the Union, despite the claims made by some critics that the Union could in this way impose economic and social policy guidelines on the Member States. The assertion in the Constitution that the Charter does not extend the field of application of Union law, does not establish any new power or task for the Union and does not modify the powers and tasks conferred on it in the Constitution (Article II-111) is particularly clear on this subject.

However, the fears held by some Member States regarding the implications of the social and economic rights recognised in the Charter prompted the Intergovernmental Conference to try to incorporate further safeguards[18] over and above those which the Convention had already laid down with a view to preventing any unwanted expansion in Union powers. The necessity of such a step, which seems to disregard well established doctrine in European constitutional law, is not clear; however, given that the legal effect of the Charter is not called into question, it can be accepted.

4.2. The rights set out in the Charter correspond, in general terms, to the common set of fundamental rights which the Union already recognised and which resulted from the constitutional traditions of the Member States or the European Convention on Human Rights. The point is that these rights should be set out in detail, in a manner readily understandable to citizens, and that it should be clearly stated that the Union is required to respect them. This can only help to strengthen citizens' trust in their Union.

4.3. The incorporation of the Charter into the Constitution is announced immediately in the opening pages of the Constitution, in a separate title (Title II of Part I) devoted to fundamental rights and Union citizenship. A further step towards the protection of fundamental rights at Union level is taken by means of the stipulation that the Union will seek accession to the European Convention for the Protection of Human Rights and Fundamental Freedoms (to which all the Member States are parties), as Parliament has long been proposing. This will entail an agreement with the Council of Europe. The decision to conclude that agreement will have to be adopted by a qualified majority, after approval by Parliament.

4.4. Further aspects of the Constitution could be cited which strengthen citizens' rights of participation in the European political process (such as the people's legislative initiative, or *citizens' initiative*: Article I-47, paragraph 4) or which help to enhance the legal protection of their rights, by facilitating access to the Court of Justice.

Parliament can only welcome these vital steps designed to transform the EU into a genuine union of States and citizens.

5. *A clear and readily understandable definition of the Union's competences*:

5.1. One of the most important questions to which the new constitutional text needed to provide an answer was that of 'who does what?' in Europe. A clarification of this kind is essential if citizens are to grasp properly the allocation of political responsibilities at European level. It will also offer an additional safeguard to all those who fear excessive intervention on the part of the Union.

5.2. With a view to providing this clarification, the Constitution defines the Union's competences, dividing them into three categories, each with a different legal status and each implying a different degree of Union intervention: the Union's exclusive competences; the competences it shares with the Member States; and action to support or complement action by the Member States. By virtue of their specific nature, the common foreign and security policy and the coordination of economic and employment policies warrant specific provisions which fall outside the three categories (cf. Annex 1).

This definition of the Union's competences is consistent with the basic principle governing the allocation of competences, i.e. that the Union enjoys only those competences which have been conferred on it by the Member States in the Constitution with a view to achieving the objectives laid down in that document. This principle is in itself sufficient to prevent the emergence of any kind of centralised superstate, since it implies that all competences rest with the States, except in those cases where they transfer them to the Union.

5.3. The Constitution does not increase the Union's competences: the small number of 'new' competences laid down correspond essentially to areas in which the Union already took action, under Article 308 of the EC Treaty, and which have been more clearly defined in the Constitution. The changes made in Part III essentially reflect the need to bring its provisions into line with the new decision-making procedures and the new legal instruments established in Part I.

5.4. In addition, the Constitution strengthens the requirement for the Union to comply with the principles of subsidiarity and proportionality when exercising its competences; monitoring of that compliance is already a matter for the Member State governments, in the Council, and Parliament. Although the definition of these principles set out by the Constitution corresponds to that already employed in the Treaties in force, the protocol on the principles of subsidiarity and proportionality provides for new mechanisms to guarantee compliance with those principles, in particular by substantially strengthening the role of the national parliaments.

5.5. Above all, the latter gain the right to be informed in good time of all Commission legislative proposals, which must be duly substantiated as regards compliance with the principles of subsidiarity and proportionality. This provision will enable the national parliaments to exercise more effectively the rights they enjoy at national level and will, in particular, enhance their ability to influence the actions of their governments in the Council of Ministers. Moreover, as regards the subsidiarity principle in particular, the national parliaments may, within six weeks following the forwarding of the proposal, send directly to the Union institutions, which must take due account of them, opinions setting out the reasons why they take the view that a proposal is not consistent with the subsidiarity principle. An 'early warning' mechanism even requires the Commission to reconsider its proposal should one-third of the national parliaments consider that the proposal in question does not comply with the subsidiarity principle.

Finally, that same protocol also offers the Member States the possibility, if the national legal system allows such provision, of bringing an action before the Court of Justice, on behalf of their national parliament or one of its chambers, against a legislative act on the grounds that it violates the subsidiarity principle. The Committee of the Regions also gains the right to bring such actions against legislative acts on which, under the Constitution, it must be consulted prior to their adoption.

These mechanisms offer further safeguards against any potentially ill-considered exercise of Union competences and will clear the way for much deeper democratic scrutiny of Community legislation.

5.6. It is true that in order to gain a full picture of the specific methods for implementing these powers the definition must be read in conjunction with the specific provisions set out in Part III of the Constitution. However, it is equally true that a simple reading of Part I will give European citizens a fairly clear insight into who does what in Europe. This represents a substantial improvement in terms of transparency.

5.7. One of the further welcome features is that the Constitution provides the system with the requisite degree of flexibility by means of a clause similar to the current Article 308 TEC, which authorises the Council, should the need arise, to adopt measures in areas where the Union has no explicit competences. This flexibility clause offers the Member States full safeguards: decision-making by unanimity and clause to be used solely in order to achieve the objectives laid down in the Constitution; the procedure to put it into effect has become more democratic, in that it is subject to approval by Parliament and the national parliaments must be notified in good time before the decision is taken.

6. *A revamped institutional framework for a stronger, more democratic and more transparent Union*

One of the key questions which the Constitution was required to resolve was that of the changes to be made to the Union institutions in order to enable them to deal with the new situation resulting from the enlargement, particularly as the Union's institutional organisation has essentially been based on the same structures for almost 50 years, even though the Union's range of tasks has expanded substantially and the number of Member States has increased from six to 25. Despite the work of a series of Intergovernmental Conferences, the key institutional issues had remained unresolved and the solutions agreed on at Nice were not satisfactory even to some of those who had negotiated them. For its part, Parliament has repeatedly drawn the attention of the public and the leaders of the Member States to the need for a radical institutional reform to endow the Union with effective, democratic and transparent institutions, whilst safeguarding the institutional balance and the Community method: the Commission which proposes legislation, Parliament and the Council which take the decisions, and the Court of Justice which guarantees the application of the texts adopted.

6.1. *European Parliament*

1. The Constitution substantially enhances the role of the European Parliament, the only European institution which directly represents citizens:

- its role as a colegislator is fully recognised, thanks to the general application of the existing codecision procedure, which is elevated to the rank of the ordinary legislative procedure, but also thanks to an increase in Parliament's participation in special legislative procedures. In future the public will have a clear perception that European law is adopted by the chamber which represents them and by the chamber which represents States; in parallel, in the field of international agreements its approval will also be required as a general rule;

- it acquires a concurrent right of initiative for revision of the Constitution and participates in the Convention procedure (its approval is required for the Council to decide not to convene the Convention);

- its budgetary powers, which it shares with the Council on an equal footing, now extend to all Union expenditure;

- its powers of political control are enhanced, particularly by means of the election of the President of the Commission;

- various decisions which are of great importance in the life of the Union and which hitherto have rested solely with the Council are now also subject to approval by Parliament: the decision to initiate enhanced cooperation; the use of the flexibility clause enabling the Union to take measures not provided for in the Constitution in order to attain ends for which it does provide; decisions on the use of the general 'bridging clauses' ('passerelles') substituting qualified majority voting for unanimous voting or replacing special legislative procedures with the ordinary legislative procedure; certain decisions making it possible to extend the scope of legal bases provided for in the Constitution, such as those concerning the European public prosecutor or judicial cooperation in criminal matters;

- even in the field of the common foreign and security policy, where it has no powers of decision, the European Parliament acquires a general right to be informed and consulted.

2. In conclusion it may be said that, despite certain fields where it might have been possible to go further, the European Parliament acquires powers of codecision in virtually all areas of Union policy. Basically, this is a matter of putting into practice the fundamental idea of the twofold legitimacy of the EU as a union of States and of citizens. Thus the Constitution undeniably represents a significant enhancement of the democratic dimension of the EU.

3. The number of Members of the European Parliament is limited to 750. The Constitution does not state how the seats are to be distributed among Member States, but instructs the European Council, on the initiative of the European Parliament and with its assent, to decide, before the 2009 elections, what its composition should be, on the basis of the principle of 'degressively proportional' representation, with a minimum of 6 and a maximum of 96 seats per Member State (the Convention proposed a minimum of 4 and no maximum). This solution will make it possible to respond more flexibly to the future development of the EU while preserving the interests of each Member State.

6.2. European Council

The European Council is recognised as an autonomous institution whose role is to impart political impetus: the Constitution expressly states that it is not to perform any legislative functions[19]. A major innovation introduced by the Constitution is the abolition of the rotating Presidency and its replacement with a President elected by the members of the European Council for a term of two and a half years, which may be renewed once. The President's duties will be to prepare and direct the work of the European Council and represent the Union externally in order to raise the Union's profile and improve the continuity and consistency of its representation, both internal and external. Provisions are included to prevent the President from exercising executive powers and to avoid any conflicts with the President of the Commission or the Minister for Foreign Affairs. Only practice will show whether these provisions are adequate.

6.3. Council

1. The key issue was that of the procedure for voting within the Council when it acts by a qualified majority. The failure of the Brussels summit in December 2003 was partly due to differences of opinion between Member States on this subject. In the view of one of the rapporteurs, the introduction of population as a criterion for both the distribution of seats in the European Parliament and votes in the Council did not guarantee a balanced system, and he expressed himself in favour of the weighted votes system for the Council. However, since the Dimitrakopoulos-Leinen report, the European Parliament had opted by a large majority for the double majority system. This is why, since the beginning of the Intergovernmental Conference, the European Parliament had insisted that a solution could only be acceptable to it if it adhered to the principle of a double majority (of Member States and the population), in order to draw attention to the twofold legitimacy underlying the development of the EU as a union of states and a union of citizens, and that the new procedure must make decision-making easier than the system provided for in the Nice Treaty.

2. It was indeed the double majority system proposed by the Convention that was finally adopted instead of weighting of votes. It may reasonably be considered that, although the thresholds have been set higher than proposed by the Convention (the Constitution now requiring 55% of States rather than 50%, and 65% of the population rather than 60%), the new system will make decision-making easier, as, in many combinations, the weighting system required far higher population thresholds for the adoption of a decision, and because, in many cases, the fact that at least four Member States will be required to form a blocking minority will have the effect of considerably reducing the 65% population threshold[20].

3. The progress made in terms of transparency and clarity of the system, on the other hand, leaves much to be desired. Certainly, the logic of the double majority is far easier to understand than any weighting of votes, but there is a risk that the public may regard the thresholds which have been adopted as rather arbitrary, and above all, the combination of different, complementary criteria greatly impairs the gains in terms of simplification and comprehension of the system[21].

4. While regretting the abandonment of the compromise arrived at by the Convention, it should be borne in mind that the solution ultimately adopted was chosen after a hard-fought battle among the Member States, the purpose of which was not always entirely clear: the impact of a few percentage points more or less on the relative degree of influence of each Member State in the voting system obscured the fact that in reality, coalitions between Member States are subject to change and are quite contingent - how many times has a decision been marked by a division between all the 'large' Member States on the one hand and all the 'small' Member States on the other? Often, the same action was intended to pursue contradictory objectives simultaneously, such as preserving a State's own opportunities to block decisions while attempting to reduce the opportunities for others to do so. And above all, the whole of this debate was carried on without considering that ultimately the dynamics of Community negotiations are such that votes are very rarely taken. Political realities being what they are, however, Parliament can accept the agreement reached between the Heads of State and of Government, albeit without concealing its regrets.

5. Whatever the method by which decisions are taken, it must be applicable. Hence the importance of the question of the field of application of qualified majority voting. The Constitution makes significant progress in this regard: there are approximately 45 new cases in which qualified majority is to apply in various fields (cf. Annex 2). On the other hand, unanimity is still required in 70 cases. While the general direction of the changes can only be regarded as

very positive, it is regrettable that the opportunity was not taken to do more in certain cases, and there were instances where the IGC even retreated from proposals on which consensus had been reached after mature reflection in the Convention (the most flagrant example being that concerning the multiannual financial framework).

6. Another major improvement made by the Constitution in terms of transparency is the requirement for meetings of the various configurations of the Council to be divided into two parts, depending on whether the Council is acting in a legislative capacity or in other ways, with the corollary that when it deliberates or votes on legislative acts, the Council meets in public. Although it can only be regretted that the Member States did not accept the Convention's proposal, which Parliament was strongly in favour of, that a genuinely separate Legislative Council should be created, it may be considered that the essential aspect of this proposal, which was that meetings should be held in public and that the Council's legislative work should be transparent, has been preserved.

7. As regards the configurations and functioning of the Council, the main novelty is the creation of an autonomous Foreign Affairs Council, to be chaired by the Minister for Foreign Affairs. This and the General Affairs Council are the only two configurations of the Council whose existence is provided for by the Constitution, which leaves it to the European Council to decide by a qualified majority on the creation of other configurations. The efforts to modify the existing system of rotating Presidencies of the Council in order to raise the profile and increase the consistency and continuity of its work have had somewhat limited results. The Member States deviated from the Convention's proposal, ultimately adopting the principle of equal rotation within a system of team Presidencies determined by a decision of the European Council, acting by a qualified majority, and it is not possible to see in advance exactly what the real benefits of this will be.

6.4. Commission

1. Another of the institutional questions which were at the centre of debate both at the Convention and at the Intergovernmental Conference was the composition of the Commission. The solution ultimately opted for, with its implementation deferred, deviated from the Convention's proposal, but it corresponds better with political reality and may be considered positive: it makes it possible to respect the new Member States' aspiration to be represented in the Commission during the first years after their accession, although in future, after a reasonable lapse of time (2014), the vital reduction in the number of Commissioners (to 2/3 of the number of Member States, which - even in a 27-member EU - would already mean that there were fewer

Commissioners than at present). Based on a rotation system which preserves equality between Member States, this solution will thus make it possible to contain the size of the Commission within acceptable limits. The frequency of the period when any given Member State will not nominate a Commissioner will be once in every three terms.

2. The Constitution makes important progress regarding the appointment of the President of the Commission, who is in future to be elected by the European Parliament on a proposal by the European Council, acting by a qualified majority. This is a further step in the process of imparting political legitimacy to the Commission, particularly as the European Council is required to take account of the elections to the European Parliament. Afterwards, the whole Commission, the President, the Minister for Foreign Affairs, who is appointed by means of a special procedure (see below), and the Commissioners, selected by the Council in agreement with the President-designate, will require a vote of approval en bloc by the European Parliament[22].

3. The enhanced role of the President of the Commission should also be noted, particularly as regards the internal organisation of the Commission and the right to demand the resignation of a Commissioner, which should improve the efficiency of the Commission.

6.5. Minister for Foreign Affairs

1. One of the main institutional novelties of the Constitution is the creation of the post of Minister for Foreign Affairs of the Union (merging in a single post the pre-existing posts of High Representative for the Common Foreign and Security Policy and Commissioner responsible for external relations), which will correspond to the objective of ensuring that all the external actions of the EU are consistent and have a high profile. Institutionally, the Minister will wear two 'hats': he will be responsible for conducting the EU's Common Foreign and Security Policy, for which purpose he will chair the Foreign Affairs Council, present proposals and implement Council decisions, while at the same time he will be a Vice-President of the Commission, taking on that institution's responsibilities in the field of external relations and coordinating all aspects of the EU's external action. He will be assisted by a European External Action Service composed of officials from the Commission, the General Secretariat of the Council of Ministers and national diplomatic services, which is to be set up by decision of the Council after consulting the European Parliament and obtaining the approval of the Commission.

2. Thus the Minister will be a member of the Commission, but he will have a special status, reflected in the procedures for his appointment and the possible ending of his tenure: he will be appointed by the European Council,

acting by a qualified majority, with the agreement of the President of the Commission; he may be dismissed by the European Council using the same procedure, and must resign if the President of the Commission asks him to do so. As a member of the Commission, his appointment must also be approved by the European Parliament when it votes on the investiture of the Commission as a whole, and if the Commission resigns en bloc following a motion of censure by the European Parliament, this also applies to him.

3. These provisions essentially correspond to what the European Parliament had long been calling for: the Minister will indeed be able to increase the consistency and efficiency of the Union's international action, promote the emergence of a genuine common foreign policy and raise the Union's international profile by giving it a 'face'. The threefold political responsibility of the Minister, to the European Parliament, the Council and the President of the Commission, is positive. But potential conflicts between the Minister and the President of the Commission or the President of the European Council remain possible, and his hybrid status may give rise to conflicts of loyalty to the Council and Commission.

6.6. The Court of Justice of the European Union

The Constitution also enhances the role of the Union's judicial wing, which it calls the '*Court of Justice of the European Union*', comprising the 'Court of Justice', the 'General Court' and possible 'specialised courts', which may be instituted by a European law[23]. Although there are no major changes in the composition and organisation of the Court of Justice and the General Court (Court of First Instance), a preliminary stage is introduced into the procedure for appointing judges and advocates-general: before being appointed by the Member States, the candidates nominated by the governments will be heard by a committee with a remit to assess the candidates' suitability to perform their duties.

In future, acts of the European Council and of the agencies will be subject to judicial control to ensure their legality. The conditions for the admissibility of complaints by natural and legal persons about regulatory acts are eased. There will be no restrictions on the bringing of actions against acts adopted in the field of judicial cooperation in criminal matters and police cooperation, except as regards reviewing the validity and proportionality of police operations and the exercise by States of their responsibilities for maintaining public order and internal security. Finally, although the acts adopted in the field of the common foreign and security policy cannot in themselves be the subject of legal proceedings, the Court nonetheless has jurisdiction to consider the legality of European decisions providing for restrictive measures again legal and natural persons.

6.7. *Other institutions and advisory bodies*

1. The provisions concerning the *European Central Bank* (elevated to the rank of an institution of the Union) and the *Court of Auditors* remain virtually unchanged. However, it may be noted that the members of the Bank's Executive Board are in future to be appointed by the Council acting by a qualified majority and no longer unanimously.

2. As regards the *Committee of the Regions* and the *Economic and Social Committee*, there are virtually no changes. However, the Committee of the Regions acquires the right to bring an action on grounds of a violation of the principle of subsidiarity by a legislative act for the adoption of which the Constitution requires it to be consulted.

* * *

It may thus be concluded that, despite certain aspects with regard to which it is not possible to judge in advance how effective the proposed changes will be, the Constitution succeeds in clarifying and enhancing the capacity of the institutions while preserving the 'Community method' and the institutional balance, which should enable the Union to respond to the new situation arising from enlargement and assert itself in the international context.

7. Acts and procedures: a more coherent, precise and comprehensible system

7.1. The Constitution brings about significant progress in terms of simplification and rationalisation of decision-making procedures and instruments for action. The gains as regards the efficiency of procedures, their democratic legitimacy and their transparency are obvious. Even the changes of terminology are important in order to allow citizens to understand more clearly who decides what in the Union and how.

7.2. The *typology of legal instruments* is simplified and clarified: six types of legal instrument are provided for: laws, framework laws, regulations, decisions, recommendations and opinions. These terms are simple and clear, and the designation 'European' added to each of these categories will make it clear to the public what is meant, since they correspond to the terminology used in most Member States (a law is a set of rules emanating from Parliament, a regulation is a set of rules adopted by the executive), putting an end to the confusion and terminological imprecision which have prevailed until now.

7.3. The Constitution also establishes a clear *hierarchy of instruments*. The supremacy of legislative acts over executive acts is clearly stipulated. The Commission is recognised as the European executive, which has the duty to take the necessary measures to implement legislative acts at European level, while the Council only exceptionally performs executive responsibilities, in the cases where the Constitution expressly so determines, or when legislative acts, stating due reasons, so specify.

7.4. The creation of a category of *delegated regulations*, which involve power being delegated by the legislative authority (the European Parliament and the Council) to the Commission, will be able to render the Union's action more efficient, as there will be no need for the legislature to concern itself with technical details which can be dealt with more quickly and appropriately by the executive; delegation of powers is accompanied by the requisite guarantees of control by the legislative authority (by means of the 'call-back' procedure), and complete equality between the European Parliament and the Council is ensured[24].

7.5. The *new legislative procedures*: the Constitution clearly places the emphasis on the *ordinary legislative procedure* (which corresponds to the existing codecision procedure); this is the legislative procedure *par excellence*, which the other types of procedure are conceived as exceptions, which must be explicitly provided for in the Constitution. The main features of the ordinary legislative procedure are as follows: the power of initiative rests with the Commission (except in the case of certain topics in the field of the area of freedom, security and justice, where the Commission shares it with at least 1/4 of the Member States), there is codecision by the European Parliament and the Council (some small changes which have been made to the old codecision procedure are intended precisely to stress the complete equality between the two institutions), and the Council adopts its decision by a qualified majority.

7.6. The scope of the ordinary legislative procedure has been substantially expanded: some fifty new legal bases (bringing the total to 86), some of which are of enormous importance, such as those concerning the area of freedom, security and justice, policy on agriculture and fisheries, the European research area and the definition of implementing powers (hitherto governed by the framework decision on comitology) or the current Financial Regulation (cf. Annex 3). In all these fields, the Council can no longer decide by itself, but only in agreement with Parliament.

7.7. Regrettably, there are still too many cases in which *special legislative procedures* apply, so that one institution adopts an act with the participation of the other institution - which may range from assent to mere consultation

- and in some cases it is difficult to see the choice of this type of procedure as anything but the result of concessions made during the negotiations at the Intergovernmental Conference. There are three cases in which the European Parliament may enact laws with the assent of the Council[25]. In contrast, there are 28 cases in which provision is made for Council laws[26]. The law containing the annual budget is subject to a special procedure for joint decision-making by the European Parliament and the Council (cf. point 8 below).

7.8. Despite these exceptions, the Constitution undeniably represents distinct progress in terms of the efficiency and democratic legitimacy of European law-making. This progress is accompanied by similar progress regarding the adoption of the international agreements concluded by the Union, thanks to the extension of the application of the qualified majority voting procedure in the Council and the requirement that the assent of the European Parliament be obtained (for example on agreements implementing the common commercial policy).

8. **The Union's finances**

8.1. One of the questions which gave rise to most debate, both at the Convention and at the Intergovernmental Conference, was reform of the Union's system of finance, particularly the budgetary procedure. It was a matter of institutionalising a system which in future would make it possible to finance the Union adequately, transparently and democratically, and particularly for the European Parliament to consolidate its powers as an arm of the budgetary authority by giving it a decisive say on the whole of the EU budget, including expenditure hitherto classified as 'compulsory', such as expenditure on the common agricultural policy and the common fisheries policy. The final result, although positive overall, to some extent represented a change of emphasis by the Intergovernmental Conference, which did not entirely accept the Convention's proposals.

8.2. The Convention had proposed a three-stage model which was simple and balanced:

- the Council would continue to decide unanimously (with the subsequent approval of the Member States in accordance with their respective constitutional rules) on the essential features and on the own-resources ceiling[27];

- the European Parliament and the Council would decide jointly on the Financial Perspective, which would be constitutionalised under the name 'multiannual financial framework' (the Council would decide by a qualified majority as from the first financial framework after the entry into force of the Constitution);

- the two institutions would decide jointly on the annual budget: after a first reading in each institution, which could lead to the convening of a conciliation committee, Parliament would have the last word in the event of disagreement, on condition that a very large majority was in favour; otherwise, the Council's position would prevail.

8.3. This meant that the Member States would continue to hold the key to the determination of the amount and nature of the Union's revenue, that the two arms of the budgetary authority would have to agree on the programming of expenditure and that, in the event of disagreement on the annual budget, the European Parliament could have the last word on overall expenditure (the distinction between compulsory and non-compulsory expenditure being dropped), albeit within the limits of the ceilings imposed by the financial framework. In practice, the two institutions would thus have been strongly encouraged to reconcile their views.

8.4. A large number of the Member States were unhappy with this balanced system, and throughout the Intergovernmental Conference proposals were submitted which in some cases even represented a serious assault on the European Parliament's existing powers in this field and ran the risk of destroying the idea of financial democracy in the Union. Thanks particularly to the efforts of the representatives of the European Parliament and the Italian and Irish Presidencies, it proved possible to find a compromise which preserves the essential aspects of Parliament's rights in this field:

- the Convention's proposals on own resources were accepted;

- the financial framework must always be adopted by the two institutions, but the Council will decide unanimously until the European Council, also acting unanimously, decides that the Council may decide by a qualified majority;

- the annual budget is also adopted jointly by the European Parliament and the Council, but in the event of disagreement the procedure must begin again with the submission by the Commission of a new draft budget.

8.5. As has already been said, this solution preserves the essential aspects of the European Parliament's budgetary powers: Parliament is given a decisive voice on the whole of budget, in view of the abolition of the distinction between compulsory and non-compulsory expenditure. But the retention of the unanimity requirement for the adoption of the multiannual financial framework will seriously complicate future negotiations on the subject and provide less encouragement for the budgetary conciliation between the institutions which was the rationale underlying the Convention's proposal.

9. Progress on sectoral policies

Part III of the Constitution, concerning 'The policies and functioning of the Union', consists of 322 articles and is the largest part. It consists almost entirely of provisions which already exist in the treaties as they stand at present concerning the definition and implementation of sectoral policies, particularly the legal bases for the Union's action in each field. It may be considered that many of these provisions could have been simplified or adjusted in the light of the changes which have occurred since they were drafted. But the fact is that the mandate which the European Council conferred on the Convention did not empower it to revise these provisions in depth.

Thus the changes made in Part III are essentially consequences of the choices made in Part I of the Constitutional Treaty regarding the abolition of the 'pillars', the powers of the Union, the institutions, decision-making procedures and legal instruments. That is why, apart from the area of freedom, security and justice (essentially the former third pillar) and external relations, particularly the common foreign and security policy, where the changes are most sensitive, in the other sectoral policies the changes mainly concern the procedures applicable and the breakdown of legal bases between legislative and non-legislative acts. This in itself may already constitute a guarantee of greater efficiency, democratic legitimacy and transparency of the Union's action in view of the positive character of the changes which we have analysed above. It may incidentally be noted that an initial chapter has been introduced which lists the horizontal or cross-cutting clauses which apply across the board to all policies. We shall review the main aspects of these changes, with the aim of determining whether they enable the Union to act more efficiently and democratically in the fields in question.

9.1. The Area of Freedom, Security and Justice

1. In the internal policy sphere, the provisions dealing with the area of freedom, security and justice are those where the greatest changes are to be found, with, in particular, the pillar structure being discontinued and judicial cooperation in criminal matters and police cooperation (which, up to now, have come under the third pillar) being brought under the 'Community' method through the extension of the ordinary legislative procedure and qualified majority

voting[28]. Specific institutional arrangements nonetheless continue to apply: the strategic guidelines for legislative and operational planning are defined by the European Council (by consensus), without Parliament being involved in any way; legislative initiative in connection with judicial cooperation in criminal matters and police cooperation is shared between the Commission and one quarter of the Member States (rather than a single Member State as is currently the case); and the national parliaments are given a larger role, particularly as regards monitoring compliance with the subsidiarity principle (one quarter of national parliaments required to trigger the early warning procedure, rather than one third).

2. The policy objectives in this area are clarified and defined more precisely. Union action is the area is explicitly made subject to compliance with fundamental rights. Access to justice is enshrined as a general objective. Mutual recognition of the various systems and the approximation of laws are recognised as two parallel means of implementing policies.

Policies on border checks, asylum and immigration are recognised as common policies of the Union, governed by the principles of solidarity and fair sharing of responsibility among Member States.

The Constitution also marks a major step forward as regards judicial cooperation in both civil and criminal matters and of police cooperation, mainly through the application of the ordinary legislative procedure.

3. *Judicial cooperation in civil matters* is extended to all matters having cross border implications and is based on the principle of mutual recognition of judgments and decisions in extrajudicial cases, with the ordinary legislative procedure applying to any measures for the approximation of laws, with the exception of measures concerning family law, in which case unanimity is the rule (Council law, with Parliament merely being consulted). However, the Council may itself decide unanimously to extend the ordinary legislative procedure to cover some aspects of family law with cross-border implications.

4. The major innovation as regards *judicial cooperation in criminal matters* is that the ordinary legislative procedure (qualified majority) is to be used for the approximation of laws covering both procedural matters (minimum rules to facilitate mutual recognition of judgments and judicial decisions, etc.) and substantive criminal law, with minimum rules concerning the definition of some serious crimes with cross-border dimensions listed in the Constitution, and sanctions. The Constitution even provides that the Council may, acting unanimously, identify other aspects of criminal procedure and other areas of crime to which the ordinary legislative procedure may apply.

Some Member States were strongly opposed to this, despite the guarantee that European legislation in this area must respect the fundamental aspects of the Member States' legal systems. Therefore, in order to secure agreement, the Intergovernmental Conference made provision for an 'emergency brake' mechanism which provided the Member States that were having problems in this area with all the guarantees they required, without completely ruling out any further progress. Under this arrangement, should a Member State consider that a legislative proposal jeopardises 'fundamental aspects' of its legal system, it can ask for the matter to be referred to the European Council. The European Council has four months in which to refer the matter back to the Council so as to enable the procedure to continue, or to request the Commission or the group of Member States that submitted the original text to submit a new legislative proposal. Should the European Council fail to take a decision within the four-month period, or should the new legislative procedure opened at its request not be completed within twelve months, enhanced cooperation shall be established in the matter automatically if one third of the Member States are in favour.

5. Parliament can also welcome the fact that the Intergovernmental Conference adopted the Convention's proposal for the establishment of a *European Public Prosecutor's Office* which has responsibility for combating offences against the Union's financial interests and may prosecute the perpetrators of such offences, despite strong opposition from several delegations. However, the Constitution stipulates that the Council law establishing the office must be adopted unanimously once Parliament has given its consent. A 'bridging clause' ('passerelle') nonetheless provides for the possible extension of the office's responsibilities to cover action to combat serious crimes with a cross-border dimension, by means of a European decision adopted unanimously by the Council after Parliament has given its consent.

6. Lastly, the ordinary legislative procedure has also been introduced for *police cooperation*, although unanimity continues to be rule for operational cooperation and intervention by the competent authorities of one Member State on the territory of another Member State.

9.2 Other internal policies

1. Aside from the introduction of a few new legal bases for 'new' - or more clearly defined - competences in Part I, the changes which the Constitution makes to the other sectoral policies stem mainly from the establishment of codecision (and thus qualified majority voting) as the ordinary legislative procedure and the breakdown between legislative and non-legislative acts as now defined.

2. Some of the most striking changes are to be found in the fields of *agricultural policy and fisheries policy*, where the ordinary legislative procedure will apply for the adoption of legislative acts laying down rules for the common organisation of agricultural markets and the other provisions required for the pursuit of the common agricultural and fisheries policies (under the current arrangements, Parliament is merely consulted). This means that the shaping of the main lines of the common agricultural and fisheries policies will become a matter to be decided by Parliament as well, and no longer just by agricultural ministers. However, the setting of prices, levies, aid and quantitative limitations and the allocation of fishing quotas are to be dealt with by means of non-legislative acts (European regulations or decisions) adopted by the Council.

3. A new strand, *space policy*, has been added to *research and technological development policy*. The research framework programme will now be enacted by a European law adopted by a qualified majority. A European research area within which researchers, scientific knowledge and technologies may move freely will be established under laws adopted under the ordinary legislative procedure. A European space programme may be adopted by means of a law or framework law. It should be noted that Parliament's legislative rights in this area were seriously called into question by some of the proposals put forward during the IGC.

4. The objectives set out in the new section on *energy* include ensuring the functioning of the energy market and security of energy supply and promoting energy efficiency and the development of renewable forms of energy. The IGC placed a limit on legislative action by the Union, which must not affect a Member State's right to determine the conditions for exploiting its energy resources, its choice between different energy sources and the general structure of its energy supply. Furthermore, although the ordinary legislative procedure and qualified majority voting are the rule in this area, the IGC stipulated that any measures primarily of a fiscal nature must be taken by means of a Council law adopted unanimously after Parliament has been consulted.

5. In the *public health* field the IGC went a little further than the Convention by adding, 'early warning of and combating serious cross-border threats to health' to 'the fight against the major health scourges' among the support measures to be taken by the Union. The Union must also, among other things, lay down measures setting high standards of quality and safety for medical products and measures to protect public health regarding tobacco and alcohol abuse. It should be emphasised that the Constitution stipulates that Union action in this area shall respect the responsibilities of the Member

States for the definition of their health policy, including the management of health services and medical care and the allocation of the resources assigned to them.

6. One can regret that the text finally agreed does not contain more substantial changes in the *social policy* field, particularly as regards the extension of qualified majority voting (no change with respect to the present situation). It would, however, be wrong to say that the Constitution represents a step backwards in this area. On the contrary, various advances are made, namely:

- inclusion of 'full employment' and 'social progress' among the Union's objectives in the opening articles of the Constitution;

- introduction at the beginning of Part III of a general 'social clause' under which, in defining and implementing all policies, the Union must take into account 'requirements linked to the promotion of a high level of employment, the guarantee of adequate social protection, the fight against social exclusion, and a high level of education, training and protection of human health';

- the establishment of a legal basis enabling services of general economic interest to be recognised and safeguarded;

- explicit recognition in Part I of the role played by the 'social partners', particularly the Tripartite Social Summit for Growth and Employment, which is to contribute to social dialogue.

Furthermore, it should not be forgotten that the incorporation of the Charter of Fundamental Rights into the Constitution means that the social rights enshrined in the charter will be fully recognised in Community law.

7. Lastly, the ordinary legislative procedure will apply to social security measures covering employed and self-employed migrant workers' entitlement to benefits. This will be combined with another 'emergency brake' mechanism, to apply in cases where a Member State considers such measures 'would affect fundamental aspects of its social security system, including its scope, cost or financial structure, or would affect the financial balance of that system'. It may then request that the matter be referred to the European Council (thus automatically suspending the legislative procedure). The European Council must then within a period of four months either refer the matter back to the Council, thus enabling the procedure to continue, or ask the Commission to submit a new proposal. (The Constitution does not, however, state what would happen should the Council fail to act.)

8. The Constitution does not make any changes to the situation as regards *taxation*, where unanimity remains the general rule. The IGC failed to agree even to the relatively limited number of cases in which the Convention proposed that the ordinary legislative procedure (i.e. qualified majority) should apply in connection with administrative cooperation measures and action to combat tax fraud and evasion (subject to the Council unanimously establishing that the proposed measures related to these issues).

9. Another area that came in for much discussion but in which the changes are relatively minor is that of *economic governance*. However, the *coordination of economic and employment policies* has been confirmed as a Union competence (although the IGC amended the Convention text to place the emphasis on the fact that the Member States coordinate their policies according to arrangements determined within the Union) and the provisions specific to Member States whose currency is the euro have been fleshed out. For example, the Council decision on the adoption of the euro by new Member States (proposed by the Commission) must be preceded by a recommendation from a qualified majority of the Member States whose currency is already the euro.

Furthermore, the operating procedures of the *Euro Group* are set out in a protocol attached to the Constitution. The IGC also adopted a Declaration on the Stability and Growth Pact. The pact was the subject of heated discussions among some delegations, resulting in the adoption of changes to the Convention text which, inter alia, have reduced the importance of the Commission's proposed role in the excessive deficits procedure (with the recommendations addressed by the Council to the Member State concerned being adopted on the basis of a Commission recommendation, as is currently the case, rather than a proposal, as the Convention was proposing).

9.3. Common foreign and security policy

1. Major changes have also been made in the external relations sphere, but more to institutional arrangements than to decision-making procedures. In keeping with the creation of the post of Minister for Foreign Affairs (*see section 6.5 above*), the holder of which will, in institutional terms, wear two 'hats' and will be responsible for conducting the common foreign and security policy and coordinating all aspects of the EU's external relations, the Constitution now brings all areas of EU external action together in a separate title (Title V of Part III).

Unanimity will continue to be the rule in the common foreign and security policy sphere, which continues to come under essentially intergovernmental procedures and in which the European Council plays the dominant role.

Qualified majority voting will apply only to the implementation of decisions taken by the European Council (or proposals submitted by the Minister at the European Council's request) or the Council. Provision has, however, been made for an 'emergency brake' in cases where a Member State opposes the adoption of a decision by a qualified majority for vital reasons of national policy. Neither the Convention's proposals (qualified majority for proposals submitted by the Minister and supported by the Commission) nor the Italian Presidency's proposals (qualified majority for all of the Minister's proposals) were adopted, owing to opposition from various Member States. Parliament has been given the general right to be informed, and in some cases consulted. The Court of Justice's jurisdiction over common foreign and security policy is limited. However, the Constitution does give the Court jurisdiction to review the legality of European decisions resulting in restrictive measures against individuals.

2. The greatest advances brought by the Constitution are to be found in the specific area of common security policy, where the Intergovernmental Conference made major changes which went even further than those proposed by the Convention.

As a result, a common defence, or at least the formulation of a common defence policy, the principles for which were already approved in the Maastricht Treaty - has become a more realistic prospect[29]. This common defence policy gives the Union an operational capacity based on civil and military assets. The main changes in this connection are:

- revision of the 'Petersberg' missions[30];

- establishment of a European Armaments, Research and Military Capabilities Agency[31];

- the option to establish, by means of a Council decision adopted by a qualified majority, permanent structured cooperation in the defence field among Member States which have the military capacity and political will to be involved (the conditions for implementing such structured cooperation are set out in a protocol annexed to the Constitution);

- a mutual aid and assistance obligation among Member States under which Member States must use all means in their power to assist a Member State that is the victim of armed aggression on its territory, in accordance with the United Nations Charter and in compliance with the NATO commitments of the Member States that are members of that organisation. The Constitution stipulates that this obligation shall not prejudice the specific character of the security and defence policy of certain Member States, which is an important guarantee for the Member States that have traditionally been 'neutral';

- with a view to protecting the values of the Union, the Council will be able to entrust the implementation of a task to a group of Member States;
- establishment of a start-up fund made up of contributions from the Member States, to cover military expenditure not charged to the Union budget,
- laying down of a procedure for rapid access to appropriations in the Union budget.

3. The Constitution also contains a solidarity clause under which the Member States must provide assistance to any Member State that is the victim of terrorist attack or natural disaster, if it so requests. The arrangements for implementing this clause will be adopted by decision of the Council, on a joint proposal from the Commission and the Minister. The Council will decide unanimously if this decision has defence implications. Parliament will be informed.

4. These advances are therefore significant and do not undermine the specific character of the security and defence policy of certain Member States or the commitments of the Member States that belong to NATO. Furthermore, they are not likely to transform the Union into an aggressive military bloc, as some people seem to fear. Some people would certainly have liked to go further, particularly as far as qualified majority voting is concerned. However, in view of the fact that this in an eminently intergovernmental policy area and of the political climate in which the Intergovernmental Conference was held, the final outcome can be considered to be relatively positive.

9.4. Other areas of external relations

1. Positive changes have been made in the area of *common commercial policy*. Its scope has been extended as regards trade in services and intellectual property. Parliament's role is enhanced: the ordinary legislative procedure will be used to lay down measures implementing the common commercial policy; and Parliament will receive regular reports on negotiations on international agreements, which may not be concluded without its consent. The Constitution also endorsed what is referred to as the 'cultural exception'[32].

2. Lastly, as regards *humanitarian aid*, Parliament can welcome the establishment of a specific legal basis coming under the ordinary legislative procedure and providing for the establishment of a voluntary humanitarian aid corps.

10. *A significant degree of flexibility*

Another question of fundamental importance is whether the new constitutional framework is sufficiently flexible to enable the Union to adjust to changing circumstances and meet new challenges that may arise in the future.

To find an answer to this question we need to address two issues: firstly, that of revision of the Constitution and secondly that of whether the system can evolve within the confines of the constitutional framework, without the need for revision of the Constitution itself.

1. The new treaty makes a number of clear improvements to the revision procedure, first and foremost among which is the granting of a right of initiative as regards revision to Parliament, on the same basis as the Member States and the Commission. It also places the Convention on an institutional footing as the body responsible for preparing revisions, in recognition of both the truly decisive role the Convention played in the drafting of the Constitution and the limitations of the intergovernmental method. Parliament, which was the first to propose that the Convention method be used, cannot but welcome this change, which will help to make the revision procedure more transparent and democratic at the same time as making it more effective.

One particularly positive development is the fact that Parliament must give its approval should the Council decide not to convene a Convention on the grounds that the changes are not sufficiently major.

2. Unfortunately, the Intergovernmental Conference did not live up to Parliament's expectations as regards simplifying the revision procedure. The text of Article IV-444 does contain a simplified procedure for revising the provisions of Title III of Part III on the internal policies of the Union (on condition that such revision does not increase the competences allocated to the Union), but this procedure merely allows the European Council to bypass the Convention method (without requiring Parliament's consent); furthermore, unanimity and ratification by all the Member States remain the rule.

3. Revision of the Constitution will thus continue to require unanimity and ratification by all the Member States in all cases. Even though various proposals were put forward which enjoyed broad support in Parliament and among the national parliaments and would have made this requirement a little more flexible as regards the revision of the provisions of Part III (which are quite detailed and many of which are of questionable constitutional value)

while complying with the fundamental principle that any further increase in the Union's competences would need to be unanimously approved by the Member States.

4. Conversely, Parliament cannot but welcome the retention of the 'bridging clauses' ('passerelles') which the Convention proposed for changes from unanimous voting to qualified majority voting within the Council or from special legislative procedures to the ordinary legislative procedure. The fact that this decision can only be taken unanimously by the European Council with Parliament's consent - and then only if no national parliament expresses any objections within a six-month period - provides an adequate guarantee that due respect will be shown for the rights of each Member State and that the decision will be transparent and democratically valid.

5. Another positive aspect of the new constitutional text is the improvements made in connection with enhanced cooperation, the importance of which may increase in future in view of the substantial increase in the number of Member States. While establishing the conditions required to ensure the overall cohesion and institutional unity of the Union, the Constitution extends the scope of enhanced cooperation (which can now apply to all areas not covered by the exclusive competences of the Union, while under the current arrangements defence policy is excluded) and facilitates their establishment. Enhanced cooperation must bring together at least one-third of the Member States, with the Council acting by a qualified majority except in common foreign and security policy matters, where unanimity will continue to be required. Furthermore, the requirement that Parliament's consent be sought (except in common foreign and security policy matters) will enhance the democratic legitimacy of the decision to establish such cooperation.

6. Lastly, the fact that the Intergovernmental Conference managed to retain the 'bridging clause' ('passerelle') proposed by the Convention, allowing a switch to qualified majority voting or the ordinary legislative procedure within the enhanced cooperation mechanism, is also a satisfactory development.

7. *Voluntary withdrawal from the Union*: for the first time in the treaties establishing the European Communities and then the Union, which - with the exception of the first treaty, which established the European Coal and Steel Community - were expressly concluded for an unlimited period but which made no provision for a collective or individual withdrawal procedure, the Constitution establishes a mechanism for 'voluntary withdrawal from the Union' (Article I-60). It must of course be acknowledged that, in the absence of any specific provisions, such a move was anyway already permissible under international treaty law. However, the fact that withdrawal is now explicitly

provided for in the Constitution both lays down detailed arrangements for dealing with such a situation and sends out the clear message that no Member State is obliged to continue to be involved in the European project if its people no longer wish it to be involved. When taken together with the provisions on enhanced and structured cooperation, this clearly demonstrates that involvement in the Union and in the furtherance of its policies is something that must be chosen freely on the basis of a genuine political commitment.

11. *Entry into force of the Constitution*

11.1. The Intergovernmental Conference was convened on the basis of Article 48 of the Treaty on European Union, which stipulates that whatever the scope of the amendments it proposes be made to the existing treaties (including their repeal, as provided for in Article IV-437 of the draft Constitution), the amendments will not come into force until they have been ratified by *all* the Member States in accordance with their respective constitutional requirements.

11.2. This means that the provisions set out in Article IV-447 of the Constitution will apply to future ratification processes only. Article IV-447 states that if, two years after the commencement of any procedure for the ratification of changes to the treaty establishing the Constitution, one-fifth of the Member States have yet to complete the procedure or have encountered difficulties in proceeding with ratification (which also covers the possibility of the text having been rejected by one or more of them), the matter will be referred to the European Council.

11.3. With a view to the ratification of the original treaty establishing the Constitution, the IGC adopted a political declaration (No 30), the terms of which are similar to those of Article IV-447 referred to above, which was incorporated in the Final Act.

11.4. In the past, in cases where problems have occurred in some Member States during the procedure for ratifying earlier treaties, the matter has of course been referred to the European Council. However, by including this provision in line with the Convention's proposals, the IGC wished to send out the political message that it would be difficult to accept that a small minority of Member States prevent the others from moving forward, particularly in view of that fact that the Constitution provides inter alia for the option of voluntary withdrawal from the Union and that of taking part in enhanced or structured cooperation, in which not all the Member States are required to be involved. Such a situation should give rise to negotiations aimed at finding a solution that takes account of not only the situation of the Member

State that is unable to ratify the Constitution but also, and above all, that of the Member States that accept it.

III. Overall assessment/recommendation to approve the Constitution

1. Given the above, Parliament's overall opinion on the outcome of the IGC which concluded in June 2004 must be firmly in favour, given that it reflects a level of ambition that few people felt would be possible to attain in the geopolitical context in which the entire exercise has been conducted since the Laeken Declaration on the Future of the European Union in December 2001[33].

2. The procedure under which the Constitutional Treaty was drafted by the Convention was unprecedented in terms of the level of participation and degree of transparency. Subsequently, the Heads of State or Government adopted the text that will be put up for ratification in all the Member States. The resulting document is the outcome of a compromise reached among various parties, namely the national governments and national parliaments, in which democratic legitimacy is vested at national level, the European Parliament and Commission, acting on behalf of the EU institutions, and citizens, both individually and through civil society organisations. However, 'compromise' does not mean an agreement on lowest common denominators. On the contrary, despite the shortcoming described above, its provisions are extremely ambitious, which is something that had appeared Utopian in the light of the political context in which the work was conducted since the Laeken Declaration set the process in motion in December 2001.

   The consolidation of the constitutional foundations of the Union and its institutional framework and the rationalisation and simplification of its instruments are capable of at last bringing stability following two decades of permanent reform.

   The stability and certainty that are a feature of all constitutional texts are complemented by provisions which both organise the development of the decision-making process and enable use to be made of enhanced and/or structured cooperation mechanisms providing the flexibility required to adjust the way in which the Union operates so as to enable it to tackle the challenges it will be facing in coming years.

   Above all, however, the Constitution enhances democracy within the European Union, fosters more effective decision-making, ensures greater clarity about who does what in the Union and the competences assigned on the one hand to the Union and on the other to the Member States. At the press conference that followed the closure of the Convention, the chairman, Mr Valéry Giscard d'Estaing, said that the European Parliament had emerged from the Convention as the winner. The rapporteurs consider the real winners to be the European public, because this Constitution represents the biggest step forward since the Treaties of Rome in 1957, because it consolidates our values and principles in a stimulating project for living together and because it provides the best means of jointly tackling today's challenges.

3. Given the above, Parliament should take a leading role in promoting and defending the Constitution and should help to foster and consolidate the political will required for it to be fully implemented. This should start with an active involvement in the debates taking place in connection with the ratification process.

[1] Entry into force: 23 July 1951.

[2] Belgium, Germany, France, Italy, Luxembourg and the Netherlands.

[3] The following countries have joined the first six: Denmark, Ireland and the United Kingdom in 1973, Greece in 1981, Spain and Portugal in 1986, Austria, Finland and Sweden in 1995, and the Czech Republic, Estonia, Cyprus, Latvia, Lithuania, Hungary, Malta, Poland, Slovenia and Slovakia in 2004.

[4] Entry into force: 1 January 1958.

[5] Luxembourg Treaty of 17 February 1986, which came into force on 1 July 1987.

[6] Signed on 7 February 1992, came into force on 1 November 1993.

[7] Signed on 2 October 1997, came into force on 1 May 1999.

[8] Signed on 26 February 2001, came into force on 1 February 2003.

[9] Signed in Rome on 29 October 2004 and should enter into force on 1 November 2006 if all the instruments of ratification have been deposited by that date.

[10] Resolutions on the preparations for the IGCs and assessing their outcomes:

- **Single European Act**

- resolution of 14 February 1984: Spinelli report and draft Treaty (OJ C 77, 19.3.1984, p. 33)
- resolutions of 16 January 1986: Planas report (OJ C 36, 17.2.1986, p. 144) and 17 April 1986 (OJ C 120, 20.5.1986, p. 96)

- **Maastricht Treaty**

- resolutions on the report by D. Martin of 14 March 1990 (OJ C 96, 17.4.1990, p. 114),

11 July 1990 (OJ C 231, 17.9.1990, p. 97)

and 22 November 1990 (OJ C 324, 24.12.1990, p. 219)

- resolution of 7 April 1992: D. Martin report (OJ C 125, 18.5.1992, p. 81)

- **Treaty of Amsterdam**

- resolutions of 17 May 1995: D. Martin/Bourlanges report (OJ C 151, 19.6.1995, p. 56) and 13 March 1996: Dury/Maij-Weggen report (OJ C 96, 1.4.1996, p. 77)

- resolution of 19 November 1997: Méndez de Vigo/Tsatsos report (OJ C 371, 8.12.1997, p. 99)

- **Treaty of Nice**

- resolutions on the Dimitrakopoulos/Leinen report of 18 November 1999 (OJ C 189, 7.7.2000, p. 222),

  3 February 2000 (OJ C 309, 27.10.2000, p. 85)

  and 13 April 2000 (OJ C 40, 7.2.2001, p. 409)

- resolution of 31 May 2001: Méndez de Vigo/Seguro report (OJ C 47E, 21.2.2002, p. 108).

11 OJ C 80, 10.3.2001, pp. 85 and 86.

12 Mention need be made here only of the Rome 'Assises' involving the national parliaments (Conference of the Parliaments of the European Community, held from 27 to 30 November 1990), the interinstitutional conferences held in parallel with the IGCs on Economic and Monetary Union and Political Union, which culminated in the drafting of the Maastricht Treaty, the participation by Parliament representatives in the work of the Reflection Group prior to the Amsterdam IGC, followed by their involvement in the proceedings of the IGC itself, and, finally, their involvement as observers in the group set up to prepare the Nice IGC.

13 Resolution of 25 October 2000 (report by Olivier Duhamel on the constitutionalisation of the Treaties), confirmed by the resolution of 31 May 2001 (Méndez de Vigo/Seguro report on the [assessment of the] Treaty of Nice and the future of the European Union).

14 The idea of adopting such a Charter, which today forms Part II of the Constitution, was first put forward by the German Council Presidency, which secured its acceptance by the Cologne European Council of 3 and 4 June 1999. The method of drafting the Charter was also laid down at that European Council meeting, then clarified at the following meeting held in Tampere on 15 and 16 October 1999. It was decided to establish a 'body' - subsequently termed 'Convention' - bringing together the four component parts of the Convention on the Future of Europe, but without the involvement of the applicant States.

15 SN 300/1/01 REV 1, Annex 1, p. 19.

16 Resolution of 16 March 2000: Duff/Voggenhuber report on the drafting of a European Union Charter of Fundamental Rights (OJ C 377, 29.12.2000, p. 329)

- Decision of 14 November 2000: Duff/Voggenhuber report on approval of the draft Charter of Fundamental Rights of the European Union (OJ C 223, 8.8.2001, p. 74)

- Resolution of 23 October 2002: Duff report on the impact of the Charter of Fundamental Rights of the Union and its future status (OJ C 300E, 11.12.2003, p. 432)

- Resolution of 29 November 2001: Leinen/Méndez de Vigo report on the Laeken European Council and the future of the Union (OJ C 153, 27.6.2002, p. 310(E))
- Resolution of 25 October 2001: Poos report on the reform of the Council (OJ C 112, 9.5.2002, p. 317(E))
- Resolution of 14 March 2002: Carnero González report on the legal personality of the European Union (OJ C 47, 27.2.2003, p. 594(E))
- Resolution of 7 February 2002: Napolitano report on relations between the European Parliament and the national parliaments in European integration (OJ C 284, 21.11.2002, p. 322(E))
- Resolution of 16 May 2002: Lamassoure report on the division of competences between the European Union and the Member States (OJ C 180, 31.7.2003, p. 493(E))
- Resolution of 17 December 2002: Bourlanges report on the typology of acts and the hierarchy of legislation in the European Union (OJ C 31, 5.2.2004, p. 126)
- Resolution of 14 January 2003: Napolitano report on the role of regional and local authorities in European integration (OJ C 38E, 12.2.2004, p. 167)
- Resolution of 24 September 2003 on the draft Treaty establishing a Constitution for Europe and the European Parliament's opinion on the convening of the Intergovernmental Conference (IGC) (OJ C 77E, 26.3.2004, p. 255).

17 The Treaty establishing the European Atomic Energy Community (EAEC/Euratom) is not, however, affected by the Constitution and will therefore remain in force alongside it, although some of its provisions have been amended by the Protocol modifying the Euratom Treaty with a view to making them compatible with the constitutional text. However, Germany, Ireland and Austria have expressed the wish, in declaration No 44 annexed to the Final Act of the IGC, that an Intergovernmental Conference be convened as soon as possible to revise the Euratom Treaty.

Besides, it has to be said that the constitutional treaty is completed by a confusing number of protocols, annexes and declarations: 36 protocols (most of which were annexed to the existing treaties and have simply been adapted to the constitutional text, for instance those on the Schengen acquis, the role of national parliaments, the principles of subsidiarity and proportionality, transition provisions concerning the institutions, structured permanent cooperation in matters of defence, etc.), two annexes (already existing, concerning the list of agriculture products and the list of countries and overseas territories) and 46 declarations. As these protocols have the same legal force as the constitutional treaty, they must also be ratified by all Member States. This is not the case for declarations, which are not legally binding.

18 Paragraph 7 of Article II-112, which refers to the explanations drawn up on the authority of the Praesidium of the Convention that drew up the Charter of Fundamental Rights and Declaration No 12 annexed to the Final Act of the IGC, which incorporates those explanations.

19 Although the role assigned to the European Council in operating an 'emergency brake' in connection with certain decisions concerning social security and judicial cooperation in criminal matters may mean that, even if it does not directly perform legislative functions (it does not participate in the adoption of legally binding rules) it may at least interfere in a virtually decisive manner in a legislative procedure - cf. below, points 9.1.4 and 9.2.7.

20 The fact that the IGC introduced the requirement that at least four Member States should vote against a proposal in order to form a blocking minority means that in some circumstances a decision could be adopted with the support of far less than 62% of the population, which is the threshold set for the population criterion in the Nice Treaty: thus a decision opposed, for example, by Germany, France and Italy would nonetheless be adopted, even though its proponents represented only about 55% of the

population, as these three Member States cannot by themselves form a blocking minority even though between them they represent almost 45% of the population of the EU (in its current 25-member form). It is necessary to bear in mind that at present the vagaries of the various possible combinations whereby it is possible to attain the minimum number of weighted votes required for a qualified majority has the effect that in many cases the required percentage of the population is substantially greater.

On the other hand, it may be hoped that raising the threshold for the number of Member States will not, in practice, have a very significant negative impact. 55% of Member States instead of half (50%) would mean that in the 25-member EU 14 Member States would be required to vote in favour instead of 13, without the additional requirement formulated by the IGC that the majority must include at least 15 Member States; the number of Member States required to prevent a decision from being adopted will now be 12 instead of 13. In practice, the possible increase in the risks of blockage due to this increase is certainly not very great. In reality, decisions are never taken with the Member States divided into two antagonistic blocs of virtually identical proportions. Moreover, the additional requirement of at least 15 Member States, referred to above, will no longer be of any independent significance once the EU has 27 or more Member States, as is likely to be the case from 2009, when the new system enters into force (in a Union with 27 members, 55% of States is in any case equivalent to 15 Member States).

21 It should also be recalled that, besides the two corrective criteria mentioned in the text (the minimum number of States required for a blocking minority (4) and the minimum number of States required for the adoption of a decision (15)), the IGC also reached agreement on a kind of revised Ioannina compromise for a transitional period (Declaration No 5 to the Final Act of the IGC): if members of the Council representing at least 3/4 of the number of Member States or of the population required to block a decision indicated their opposition to the adoption of a Council act by a qualified majority, the Council would continue to debate the subject with a view to reaching wider agreement within a reasonable period. This agreement was formalised in a draft decision which the European Council approved. This decision will remain in force at least until 2014, when the Council could revoke it. It should also be recalled that the Constitution provides that when an initiative from the Commission is not required, or when a decision is not adopted at the initiative of the Minister for Foreign Affairs, the required qualified majority is to be bigger: 72% of Member States (as against the 2/3 proposed by the Convention), representing 65% of the population (as against the 60% proposed by the Convention).

22 It may be noted that the IGC did not accept the Convention's proposal that the government of each Member State should submit a list of three names from which the President would choose the Commissioner proposed by the Member State. Also, it is regrettable that the IGC did not accept the Commission's proposal that the investiture of the Commission should conclude with the vote by the European Parliament, which is politically highly symbolic, but added a stage to the procedure, which is now to conclude with the appointment of the Commission by the European Council, acting by a qualified majority.

23 Adopted by Parliament and the Council by means of the ordinary legislative procedure, either on a proposal from the Commission and after consulting the Court of Justice, or at the request of the Court of Justice and after consulting the Commission.

24 Each of the two arms of the legislative authority may revoke the delegation decision at any time; in addition, a delegated regulation proposed by the Commission can enter into force only if neither of the two institutions makes objections within the time limit provided for by the law or framework law delegating the power of regulation.

25 The law laying down the Statute for Members of the European Parliament, the law determining the status of the European Ombudsman and the law determining the procedures for the exercise of the right of inquiry (which likewise requires the assent of the Commission) - cf. Annex 4.

26 In 22 of these cases, the Council decides unanimously (in five cases with the assent of the European Parliament, in 17 after mere consultation); in six cases it decides by a qualified majority (in one case with the assent of the European Parliament, in five cases after mere consultation) - cf. Annex 4.

[27] The Constitution provides for a Council law, on which Parliament may only deliver an opinion. The Convention, on the other hand, proposed that the measures for the implementation of the own-resources system should be adopted by a Council law adopted by a qualified majority, with the approval of Parliament.

[28] The Constitution does not affect the special situation applying to the United Kingdom, Ireland and Denmark in connection with the area of freedom, security and justice, as set out in several existing protocols which have been adapted to the new constitutional text.

[29] The decision to establish, in time, a common defence will be taken by the European Council, acting unanimously, and will require the approval of all the Member States in accordance with their constitutional procedures.

[30] To add operations relating to disarmament, military advice, post-conflict stabilisation and the fight against terrorism, including in the territory of third countries, to the existing humanitarian and rescue tasks, conflict prevention and peace-keeping tasks and tasks of combat forces in crisis management, including peacemaking.

[31] Whose main responsibility is to promote the rationalisation of the military capacities of the Member States, the coordination of defence technology research and more effective military spending.

[32] The Constitution states that the Council shall act unanimously for the negotiation and conclusion of agreements in the field of trade in cultural and audiovisual services, where these risk prejudicing the Union's cultural and linguistic diversity. The IGC extended this 'exception' to cover the trade in social, education and health services where such agreements risk seriously disturbing the national organisation of such services and prejudicing the responsibility of Member States to deliver them. The Council shall also act unanimously where agreements in the fields of trade in services in general and the commercial aspects of intellectual property include provisions for which unanimity is required for the adoption of internal rules.

[33] Presidency conclusions, European Council meeting in Laeken, 14 and 15 December 2001 (Council doc. SN 300/1/01 REV 1).